# DISAPPEARANCES

Ann Weil

Chicago, Illinois

© 2008 Raintree
Published by Raintree,
A division of Reed Elsevier Inc.
Chicago, Illinois

Customer Service  888-454-2279

Visit our website at www.heinemannraintree.com

Designed by Victoria Bevan, Steve Mead,
and Bigtop
Printed and bound in China by Leo Paper Group

12 11 10 09 08
10 9 8 7 6 5 4 3 2 1

**Library of Congress
Cataloging-in-Publication Data**
Weil, Ann.
  Disappearances / Ann Weil.
     p. cm. -- (Atomic)
  Includes bibliographical references and index.
  ISBN 978-1-4109-2977-8 (library binding -
hardcover) ---ISBN 978-14109-2998-3 (pbk.)
  1. Disappearances (Parapsychology)--Juvenile
literature. 2.  Curiosities and wonders--Juvenile
literature.  I. Title.

  BF1389.D57W45 2007
  001.94--dc22
                              2006101211

**Acknowledgments**
The author and publisher are grateful to the
following for permission to reproduce copyright
material: Alamy Images pp. **14** (Didier Oyhenart),
**25** (Greg Vaughn), **29** bottom (CanStock Images);
Corbis pp. **5** (Bettmann), **6** (Horace Bristol),
**11** (Onne van der Wal), **13** (Hulton-Deutsch
Collection), **22** (Anthony West); Getty Editorial/
Keystone p. **10**; Getty Images pp. **17** bottom,
**18** (Hulton Archive), **29** top (Taxi); Mary Evans
Picture Library p. **9**; Popperfoto p. **17** top; The Art
Archive p. **21**; Topfoto/UPPA p. **26** top; Topham
Picturepoint p. **26** bottom.

Cover photograph of a telephone reproduced by
permission of Corbis/Zefa/Josh Westrich.

Photo research by Mica Brancic
Illustrations by Jeff Edwards

The publishers would like to thank Nancy Harris,
Dee Reid, and Diana Bentley for their assistance in
the preparation of this book.

Every effort has been made to contact copyright
holders of any material reproduced in this book.
Any omissions will be rectified in subsequent
printings if notice is given to the publishers.

**Disclaimer**
All the Internet addresses (URLs) given in this book
were valid at the time of going to press. However,
due to the dynamic nature of the Internet, some
addresses may have changed, or sites may have
changed or ceased to exist since publication. While
the author and publishers regret any inconvenience
this may cause readers, no responsibility for any
such changes can be accepted by either the author
or the publishers.

# Contents

Some words are printed in bold, **like this**. You can find out what they mean in the glossary. You can also look in the box at the bottom of the page where the word first appears.

# VANISHED!

History is full of mysterious disappearances. People vanish without a trace, and planes or ships drop out of sight and are never found. Some of these disappearances are explained by evidence. Others are based on **hearsay**, with no facts to support what happened.

## Amelia Earhart

In 1932 U.S. pilot Amelia Earhart flew an airplane **solo** across the Atlantic Ocean. In 1935 she was the first person to fly solo from Hawaii to California. Then, in 1937, she attempted to **circumnavigate** the globe. Her plan included landing on Howland Island in the South Pacific Ocean to refuel. She never made it. Search teams found no trace of her plane or of the bodies of Earhart and her navigator, Fred Noonan. What happened to them? No one knows.

| | |
|---|---|
| circumnavigate | travel all the way around something by plane or ship |
| hearsay | information heard from other people, which may or may not be true |
| solo | alone, by oneself |

The story of Earhart's last flight is one of history's most famous disappearances.

North Pole +

ARCTIC OCEAN

N. Ireland

EUROPE

ASIA

NORTH AMERICA

Newfoundland

California

ATLANTIC OCEAN

Miami

PACIFIC OCEAN

Hawaii

PACIFIC OCEAN

AFRICA

SOUTH AMERICA

Howland Island ?

New Guinea

INDIAN OCEAN

AUSTRALIA

N
W  E
S

---------- Solo flight in 1932
- - - - - - Solo flight in 1935
— — — Last flight in 1937

SOUTHERN OCEAN

South Pole + ANTARCTICA

The map shows the routes of Earhart's solo flights, and her last flight in 1937.

The Bermuda Triangle is in the Atlantic Ocean—but people do not agree exactly where it is located or how large an area it covers.

UNITED STATES
OF AMERICA

Bermuda

Miami

Gulf of
Mexico

**Bermuda
Triangle**

ATLANTIC
OCEAN

Puerto Rico

Caribbean Sea

0    1,000 miles

0    1,000 kilometers

**Flight 19 is known
as the Lost Patrol.**

# THE BERMUDA TRIANGLE AND FLIGHT 19

In 1945 five U.S. bomber planes were on a training mission called Flight 19 in an area known as the Bermuda Triangle.

## Lost without a trace

The planes took off from Fort Lauderdale, Florida, and headed out over the Atlantic Ocean. No one expected anything unusual to happen, yet the 14 men on this mission never returned. Neither did the 13 men sent out to search for them.

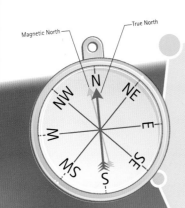

Magnetic North | True North

## Compass fact!

Compasses always point to magnetic north. The difference between magnetic north and "true north" is usually quite big. But in the Bermuda Triangle, due to the curvature of the Earth, compasses pointing to the magnetic north will also line up exactly with "true north." No wonder pilots and ship captains get lost!

## What's going on in the Bermuda Triangle?

Some people believe that aliens from outer space were behind the disappearances. Others are convinced that the lost planes and ships were sucked into a kind of **vortex** and transported to another time and place. Still, there are more reasonable explanations for the disappearances.

The Bermuda Triangle is the deepest point of the Atlantic Ocean. This might explain why some planes and ships that disappear in this area are never seen again. Bad weather, lack of experience, and strong currents could all contribute to being "lost at sea."

### Wild theories!

The Bermuda Triangle is famous for many strange disappearances. Some explanations for these are pretty wild, including alien kidnappings, portals leading into other dimensions, and time travel.

| | |
|---|---|
| dimension | level or space that something occupies |
| portal | entrance or doorway |
| vortex | large mass of swirling water or air, like a whirlpool or tornado, that can pull things inside |

JUNE

# AMAZING STORIES

25 CENTS
IN CANADA 30 CENTS

Scientifiction
Stories by

A. Hyatt Verrill
John W. Campbell, Jr.
Edmond Hamilton

Many books have been written about strange events in the Bermuda Triangle.

Last voyage of Mary Celeste

N
W E
S

New York
Azores ?

UNITED STATES OF AMERICA

Bermuda

Gulf of Mexico

Bermuda Triangle

ATLANTIC OCEAN

Caribbean Sea

0      1,000 miles
0      1,000 kilometers

The *Mary Celeste* was a two-masted sailing ship called a brigantine.

# THE MARY CELESTE

The Mary Celeste set sail from New York City on November 7, 1872. On board the ship were Captain Benjamin Spooner Briggs, his wife, their two-year-old daughter, and eight crew members.

One month later, another ship found the Mary Celeste deserted in the Atlantic Ocean near the Azores. All the passengers and one lifeboat were missing, but the **cargo** and personal belongings were left behind. The boat had obviously been abandoned quickly, and few supplies had been taken onto the lifeboat. What happened on the Mary Celeste remains a mystery.

## Abandoned!

In August 2006 an abandoned yacht was found adrift off the coast of Italy in the Mediterranean Sea. There was no name on the vessel and no way to identify it. On board were a half-eaten meal, clothing, and maps of the area. No one has ever been able to name the boat, or its owners.

| cargo | load of goods carried over land, sea, or air |

# A Cloud of Mystery

## During World War I (1914–1918), a strange event took place in Gallipoli, Turkey.

### Where did they go?

According to three New Zealand soldiers, in 1915 an English **regiment** marched into a thick fog on a hillside in Suvla Bay, Turkey. When the fog lifted, the English soldiers had disappeared!

At first, people thought the Turkish army had captured the soldiers. After the war, the British government requested that these prisoners of war be returned. But the Turkish government denied having ever captured them.

What became of these soldiers? The most likely explanation is that the witnesses were mistaken or confused. Wartime is stressful and memories are not always reliable—especially after 50 years, which is how long it took the soldiers to tell their story.

AEGEAN SEA

Suvla Bay

Gallipoli

**T U R K E Y**

0        10 miles

0        20 km

**regiment**   **group of soldiers**

The whole regiment of soldiers just disappeared into the fog.

Was David Lang "beamed up" into a UFO by aliens?

## Mark on the ground

Months after Lang vanished, the grassy area where he disappeared turned yellow. Lang's children reported hearing their father's faint cries for help, but then his voice totally faded away.

# THE LEGEND OF DAVID LANG

**On a farm in Tennessee in September 1880, in full view of several witnesses, David Lang disappeared as he was walking across a field.**

## Poof! He's gone!

The witnesses, including the man's two young children, rushed to the spot. They were convinced he must have fallen into a hole, but there was no hole. Everyone searched for him, but no trace of his body was ever found.

Did aliens in an invisible **UFO** kidnap David Lang? A more reasonable explanation is that David's "disappearance" may have been taken from a short story published in a fiction magazine—or from a **tall tale** told among friends.

| | |
|---|---|
| tall tale | story that is probably not true |
| UFO | short for Unidentified Flying Object |

# ANASTASIA ROMANOV

In 1918, after the Russian Revolution, the Russian royal family was under house arrest. Nicholas Romanov had been the tsar of the Russian Empire. Now, he, his wife Alexandra, and their five children were prisoners.

## Brutal murders

On the night of July 16, 1918, the Romanovs were told to dress for a family portrait. As the family sat and posed, soldiers opened fire. Nicholas and Alexandra were probably killed instantly, but their daughters had diamonds and other jewels sewn into their clothing. At first this repelled the bullets, but the soldiers used **bayonets** to finish the grisly murders.

However, the body of the youngest daughter, Anastasia, was never found. Had she been spared? Did she escape? Or was she killed with the others and her body was simply never identified?

| | |
|---|---|
| bayonet | long, sharp blade at the end of a rifle |
| house arrest | kept prisoner in one's own house |
| Russian Revolution | violent revolt that ended rule by the Russian royal family |
| tsar | Russian king |

The Romanov family in 1913. Anastasia is seated on the right.

Many women have claimed to be the missing Anastasia. Anna Anderson (right) was the most famous of these. She was recently proved to be a fraud.

A baby is baptized in Roanoke Island. The planters hoped for a better life than they'd had in England.

UNITED STATES OF AMERICA

N
W E
S

NORTH CAROLINA

Roanoke Island

ATLANTIC OCEAN

0        100 miles

0        200 kilometers

# THE LOST COLONY

In 1587 more than 100 men, women, and children arrived from England and settled on Roanoke Island, off the coast of North Carolina (see the map). The men were known as planters. They were given land of their own to farm.

### Left alone in a new land

The planters and their families knew their life would be difficult, especially at the beginning. They would be isolated from other Europeans and totally dependent on one another for survival.

The governor of the new **colony** returned to England with the **fleet** that had brought them all there. He was supposed to bring back more supplies for the planters and their families. What became of the planters and their families after he left is a mystery.

| | |
|---|---|
| colony | early settlement in North America |
| fleet | group of ships traveling together |

## What happened?

The governor returned to Roanoke Island three years later. It was clear that the colony had been abandoned for well over a year.

Then, the governor discovered the word "CROATOAN" carved into a tree. He thought this meant the colony had moved to Croatoan Island, off North Carolina. However, bad weather prevented him from sailing there.

Years passed and the search for the planters and their families continued without success. They were never found. To this day, no one knows for sure what happened to them.

### Inuit mystery

In November 1930 everyone in an Inuit village in northern Canada vanished. Investigators found no footprints in the deep snow, and sled dogs were buried under a high snowdrift. The Inuit left everything behind, including their food. Oddly, Inuit graves had been emptied. What happened is a mystery.

**Inuit** native people of northern Canada and other arctic regions

Did the planters move to Croatoan Island? Nobody knows for sure.

CANADA
UNITED STATES

VERMONT

0    50 miles
0    50 kilometers

▲Glastenbury Mountain
•Bennington

CANADA

VERMONT

UNITED STATES OF AMERICA

MEXICO

The map on the left shows the area in Vermont known as the "Bennington Triangle."

# THE BENNINGTON TRIANGLE

A series of unexplained disappearances near Bennington, Vermont, have earned that area the name the "Bennington Triangle," after the mysterious Bermuda Triangle.

## A guide is gone, 1945

On a mild November day in 1945, Middie Rivers led four hunters up Glastenbury Mountain in Vermont. Rivers was a fit man in his seventies, and knew the area well. As they returned to their camp, the hunters lost sight of Rivers. He was never seen or heard from again.

## A college student vanishes, 1946

On December 1, 1946, an 18-year-old college student named Paula Welden went hiking near Glastenbury Mountain. Other hikers saw her on the trail, but Welden never returned. Search teams **scoured** the area but found no trace of her, dead or alive.

**scour**  search, look for

## A hiker is missing, 1950

In October 1950 Frieda Langer and her cousin were hiking near Glastenbury Mountain when Frieda fell into a stream. She headed back to their camp to change her clothes. However, Langer never made it back to the camp. People searched for her without success.

Then, in May 1951, Langer's body was found. However, no cause of death could be determined. One witness reportedly said that the body had not **decomposed**. It was as though Langer had dropped dead that day and not seven months earlier—"like she had died of fright," the witness said.

## "Bigfoot" monster—or serial killer?

So, what was behind the Bennington Triangle disappearances? Some people claimed to have seen a Bigfoot-like creature that became known as the Bennington Monster. Others thought that there might have been a **serial killer** on the loose during the years around 1945 to 1950. No more disappearances were reported in the Bennington Triangle after 1950.

| | |
|---|---|
| **decompose** | **rot or decay** |
| **serial killer** | **murderer who kills over and over again** |

# Cursed mountain?

Native Americans believed that Glastenbury Mountain was cursed because all four winds met there. They used it only as a burial ground. Another legend about the mountain tells of an enchanted stone that swallows anything that steps on it.

All the disappearances on Glastenbury Mountain happened in the fall and early winter. Low cloud and snow showers made searching for the victims difficult.

This photo shows Lord Lucan and his wife in happier times. Did he commit **suicide** after the murder—or did he change his identity and go into hiding?

This is a photograph of Sandra Rivett, the murdered nanny.

# LORD LUCAN

## In 1974, Lady Lucan was living in London with her three children and their nanny. She had separated from her husband, Lord Lucan.

On the evening of November 8, Lady Lucan and the nanny were watching television. The nanny went downstairs to make tea, and never returned. Lady Lucan went to check on the nanny. It was dark and the light switch did not work.

### Brutal attack

Suddenly, Lady Lucan was attacked. She fought back and managed to get out of the house to summon help. When police arrived, they found the nanny murdered. The children were upstairs unharmed.

Lady Lucan claimed that her husband had come to the house to murder her—but he had killed the nanny by mistake. The police tried to track Lord Lucan down, but all they found was his abandoned car near a British harbor. Lord Lucan had disappeared. He has never been seen again since. In 1999 Lucan was eventually declared dead even though his body was never found.

**suicide**   to kill oneself

# THE MYSTERIES CONTINUE

Some people believe that very strange things are possible. Still the question remains: what really happened to all the people in this book?

## Campers vanish

In England there is a famous circle of ancient, mysterious stones called Stonehenge. In August 1971 some friends camped out near Stonehenge during a powerful thunderstorm. Two other people saw the huge stones light up with an eerie, bright blue light. They heard screams. They rushed over, but the campers had disappeared without a trace.

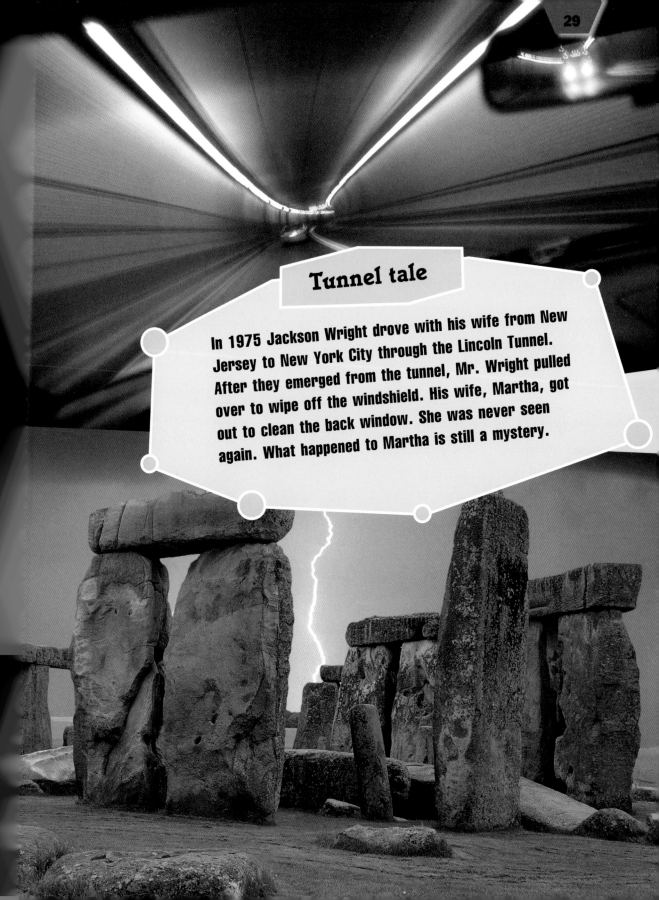

## Tunnel tale

In 1975 Jackson Wright drove with his wife from New Jersey to New York City through the Lincoln Tunnel. After they emerged from the tunnel, Mr. Wright pulled over to wipe off the windshield. His wife, Martha, got out to clean the back window. She was never seen again. What happened to Martha is still a mystery.

# Glossary

**bayonet** long, sharp blade at the end of a rifle

**cargo** load of goods carried over land, sea, or air

**circumnavigate** travel all the way around something by plane or ship

**colony** early settlement in North America

**decompose** rot or decay

**dimension** level or space that something occupies

**fleet** group of ships traveling together

**hearsay** information heard from other people, which may or may not be true

**house arrest** kept prisoner in one's own house

**Inuit** native people of northern Canada and other arctic regions

**portal** entrance or doorway

**regiment** group of soldiers

**Russian Revolution** violent revolt that ended rule by the Russian royal family

**scour** search, look for

**serial killer** murderer who kills over and over again

**solo** alone, by oneself

**suicide** to kill oneself

**tall tale** story that is probably not true

**tsar** Russian king

**UFO** short for Unidentified Flying Object. A spacecraft built and flown by beings from another planet.

**vortex** large mass of swirling water or air, like a whirlpool or tornado, that can pull things inside

# Want to Know More?

## Books

✴ Kent, Zachary. *In American History: The Mysterious Disappearance of Roanoke Colony in American History*. Enslow, 2004.

✴ Netzley, Patricia D. *The Mystery Library: The Disappearance of Amelia Earhart*. Lucent Books, 2005.

✴ Townsend, John. *Freestyle: Out There? Mysterious Disappearances*. Chicago: Raintree, 2005.

## Website

✴ www.crystalinks.com/bermuda_triangle.html
Search the site for information on the Bermuda Triangle, aliens, and UFOs.

### If you liked this Atomic book, why don't you try these...?

# Index